Sock Monkey
& FRIENDS

Sock Monkey
& FRIENDS

9 different fun-to-make sock animal projects

By Samantha Fisher
Illustrated by Cary Lane
Photos by Carlo Silvio

chronicle books · san francisco

With thanks to our families, George, Darrin, Nona,
Adrienne, Ken, Fanter, and Finn, and to the Wolf Pack,
Dragons, and Snowy Owls of the Van Zandt valley.

Text © 2010 by Samantha Fisher.
Illustrations © 2010 by Cary Lane.
Photos © 2010 by Carlo Silvio.

Design by Natalie Davis.
A **MONKEY SOCK MONKEY** book.
Typeset in Geometric 415 BT Lite.
The illustrations in this book were rendered
in gouache with digital collage.
ISBN 978-0-8118-7120-4

Manufactured by Leo Paper Products,
Heshan, China, in April 2011.

10 9 8 7 6 5 4 3

This product conforms to CPSIA 2008,
ASTM, and EN-71 safety standards.

Chronicle Books LLC
680 Second Street
San Francisco, California 94107

www.chroniclekids.com

Contents

Introducing FINNOOLA PEACH,
Sock Monkey at Large, and Eight of Her Closest Sock Friends

Finnoola Peach is the latest branch of the sock monkey family tree. Her bright-orange stripes make her a thoroughly modern monkey. She loves to travel, and she makes friends wherever she goes. This book contains step-by-step instructions for making Finnoola and eight of her sock animal pals.

Most of these sock animals are made from one pair of socks—old or new, plain or striped, argyle or whatever else inspires you. Some animals can be made from just one sock. Is that red polka-dot sock lying in the bottom of the drawer destined to stay lonely and unused, or will it become a one-sock wonder squirrel? Only you can decide!

If you already know how to sew: you're ready to get started! If you don't: that's OK, too. Basic hand-sewing instructions are included so that you can teach yourself. Or ask a friend or family member with sewing skills to help you, and make an afternoon of it together. Maybe you could make cookies to thank this nice person. If you don't know how to bake cookies, well, that's a different book.

The patterns and techniques in this book are meant to guide you, but if you have a better idea, use it. You're the boss of these socks. Now get out there and sew!

*Please introduce us to your new sock friends! Add photos of the animals you sew to the **Sock Friends Gallery** at* http://monkeysockmonkey.com.

Know Before You Sew
ABOUT THE THINGS YOU'LL NEED

Socks

Sock animals can be made from any kind of socks. Great socks can be found at your local kids' clothing boutique or shoe shop. Online, you can find most of the striped socks used in this book at http://monkeysockmonkey.com, or check http://sockdreams.com for an inspirational selection. The patterns in this book are designed for mid-calf socks, so be sure the socks you use are at least that long.

Fabric Pencil

It is helpful but not necessary to draw the patterns on the socks before you start sewing. Fabric stores sell special fabric pencils that easily wash off fabric. White chalk works, too.

Scissors, Needle, and Thread

If you don't want your stitches to show, use thread that is the same color as your sock, or a bit lighter. If you want a patchwork look where your stitches really show, try sewing with embroidery floss in a contrasting color. Any needle should work as long as the eye of the needle is big enough to fit the thread.

Stuffing

This kit contains enough polyester stuffing for one sock monkey or another two-sock friend. You can get additional stuffing at fabric or craft stores. Or look around your home! Old rags, fabric scraps, cotton balls, and many other household items make good stuffing. Do you want a crinkly monkey? Stuff it with plastic grocery bags!

When you are stuffing your animal, keep in mind that it works best to use lots of little pieces of stuffing, rather than one big piece. Use a pencil or the handle of a wooden spoon to help push stuffing into small spaces.

Buttons and Other Eyes

You can find buttons in many places. Nice shirts often come with extra buttons. You might find buttons in the bottom of your junk drawer. Or you might take your finished animal to the fabric store and find the perfect eyes on the button rack. Other ideas for eyes include sequins, beads, pearls, snaps, macaroni, subway tokens, and soft eyes made from felt or embroidery floss.

Important! Don't sew hard eyes on animals you are making for a child under the age of three. Instead, stitch on felt circles or decorate with satin stitches or knots made from embroidery floss.

SEWING BASICS

Hand Sewing versus Machine Sewing

You do not need a sewing machine to complete any of these animals. If you do have a sewing machine, it can make quick work out of sewing the outlines of the pieces, but you will still need to hand sew the stuffed pieces together.

Threading Your Needle

1. Cut a length of thread about 20 inches (50 cm) long.
2. Make sure one end of your thread is trimmed neatly.
3. Poke that end into the eye of the needle.
4. Pull the thread until the two ends meet. Tie a knot.

Knots

Starting Knot

When you stitch in stretchy knit fabric (like socks), it is a good idea to anchor your thread to the fabric itself, rather than just tying a knot in the thread. This prevents the stitches from unraveling out of the fabric. Here's one way to do that:

1. Sew into the fabric at your starting place. Leave the tail end of your thread with the knot sticking out a bit. (Try to leave the knot in a hidden spot.)

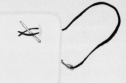

2. Pass your needle back through the fabric and then through the loop in your thread where the knot is. Gently pull the thread tight.

3. Make another stitch right next to and parallel to the first. Your needle should emerge on the same side of the fabric as the knot.

4. Pass the needle under the two stitches and let the thread form a small loop. (Don't pull it completely tight.)

5. Run the needle through this loop and pull the thread snug.

6. Repeat steps 4 and 5.

Ending Knot

Finish your stitches by making an extra stitch almost on top of your last one. Then follow steps 4 through 6, above, to tie a knot. To hide the end of the thread, poke the needle back into your animal and pull it out an inch or so away. Pull the thread taut and then cut it off about ¼ inch (6 mm) from the surface. The thread should disappear back into the body of your animal; you can stretch the fabric a bit to help the thread sink into the body, if needed.

Important! *Leave plenty of thread to tie an ending knot. When you have about 3 inches (7 cm) of thread between your needle and the fabric, tie an ending knot. Then rethread your needle and start sewing again, if necessary!*

Stitches

A few basic stitches are used in the projects in this book, and we explain how to do these stitches below. Always begin with a starting knot. Finish with an ending knot and then cut the thread (unless the instructions say not to).

Backstitch

These backstitches are playing leapfrog! Each stitch starts behind the previous and then jumps in front.

1. Poke the needle down into the fabric about 1/16 inch (2 mm) behind your starting knot, if possible.
2. Push it back up through the fabric about 1/8 inch (4 mm) forward.
3. Aim the needle back 1/16 inch (2 mm). Poke the needle back down through the fabric between the two stitches.
4. Push the needle back up 1/8 inch (4 mm) in front of your stitch.
5. Repeat this pattern of 1/16 inch (2 mm) backward, needle down, and 1/8 inch (4 mm) forward, needle up, until your line of stitches is done.

Overhand Stitch

These stitches look much like the stitches on Frankenstein's monster. They're good for sewing two stuffed parts together, like an arm and a body.

1. From your starting knot, make a stitch over the seam between the two pieces. For neatness, the stitch should be perpendicular to the seam.
2. Now sew under the seam at a slight angle. Pull the needle out just a bit past where you started.
3. Continue in the same manner. Stitches visible on the outside of the fabric should be short and straight. Diagonal stitches are hidden.

Running Stitch

In running stitches, the thread acts like a curtain rod. You can scrunch the fabric along the thread to create little folds if needed.

1. Poke the needle into the fabric and then out of the fabric 1/8 inch (4 mm) ahead of where you started.
2. Leave 1/8 inch (4 mm) space between stitches.
3. Repeat!

Satin Stitch

Satin stitches fill an area with embroidery floss. You can use satin stitches to make eyes or other details on your animals.

1. Figure out the shape you want to fill in.
2. Pull the needle through the fabric at your starting point.
3. Push it back through on the far edge of the space you are filling in. Point it back toward your first stitch.
4. Pull the needle back through the fabric, very close to where you started in step 2.
5. Push it back in very close to where you inserted the needle in step 3.
6. Continue in this way until you have filled in the shape.

How to Sew Button Eyes

The thread will be visible on the front of most buttons, so choose wisely.

1. Tie a starting knot right where the eye will be.
2. Poke the needle through the back of the button. Hold the button near the fabric.
3. Bring the needle back down through a different buttonhole.
4. Poke the needle back down into the fabric close to the start-ing knot, then pull it up out of the fabric.
5. Pull the thread so the button is tightly attached.
6. Repeat steps 2 through 5 until all of the holes in the button have been sewn through a few times.
7. Tie an ending knot behind the button.

Blink, blink! If you leave the thread tails of your starting and ending knots long when you are sewing on the button eyes, your animal will have little eyelashes.

Whew! Did you get all that? When you're working on your projects, you can refer to these instructions if you need to, or you can invent new ways of doing things as you go along. And if something seems difficult along the way, just work at it. You'll get it! Remember, when the sewing gets tough, the tough keep sewing.

FINNOOLA PEACH
Sock Monkey

This gregarious monkey spends her favorite hours visiting friends near and far. She records her journeys in her many sketchbooks. You can use the two orange-striped socks in your kit to make Finnoola, or you can find two other socks that look monkey-riffic.

You'll need

- Two socks
- Stuffing
- Scissors, needle, and thread
- Two buttons

DIFFICULTY: *Medium*

SOCK ONE

- – – – = sew line
——— = cut line

1. Turn the first sock inside out. Lay the sock flat with the heel facing up.

2. To make your monkey's legs, use the **backstitch** (see page 10) to sew through both layers of the sock, following the route shown in the picture. (It can be helpful to draw the pattern on your sock first.) Leave enough space between the leg seams for easy cutting, and don't sew all the way up to the heel.

legs

3. Cut between the legs to separate them. Be careful not to cut your stitches!

4. Turn the sock over, so the heel faces down. *Through the top layer only,* make a short horizontal cut where your monkey's mouth will be. Later, you'll sew your monkey's muzzle on top of this hole, so leave plenty of room for the eyes above it.

5. Now turn the sock right side out through the hole you just cut.

6. Add stuffing through this hole. Is your monkey skinny (loosely stuffed) or a bit more plump (firmly stuffed)? You decide!

7. Use the **overhand stitch** (see page 10) to sew the hole shut.

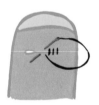

Sock Two

8. Turn the second sock inside out.

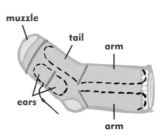

9. To make your monkey's arms, tail, and ears, use the backstitch to sew through both layers of the sock, following the route shown in the picture.

10. Cut off the toe portion of the sock about 2 inches (5 cm) in from the tip. Turn the toe right side out. This will be your monkey's muzzle.

11. Place the toe over the mouth hole in Sock One just where you think your monkey's muzzle should be. Use the overhand stitch to attach the muzzle to the body, folding the muzzle fabric edge under as you sew. Try not to sew the muzzle too flat— you want to leave room for stuffing. Sew about three quarters of the way around, and then pause.

12. Stuff the muzzle, then finish sewing it on.

13. Cut out the arms. Turn them right side out, and then stuff them.

14. Position your monkey's arms on the sides of the body, slightly lower than the muzzle. Use the overhand stitch to attach each arm to the body, folding the fabric edge under as you sew.

15. Cut the tail out. Turn it right side out, and then stuff it.

16. Put your monkey's tail on the back of the body by the heel of the sock. Use an overhand stitch to attach the tail, folding the fabric edge under as you sew.

17. Sew on your monkey's eyes just above the muzzle, following the button eye–sewing instructions on page 11. Are your monkey's eyes wide set or close together? Are they big or are they teensy-weensy?

18. Cut the ears out of the sock. Turn them right side out. Use the overhand stitch to sew them shut, folding the fabric edges in as you sew to create a tidy seam.

19. Position the ears on the sides of the head, about level with the eyes. Hold an ear flat to the head, with the rounded edge pointed forward. Use the overhand stitch to attach the ears.

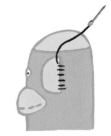

20. Now your monkey is complete! Adorn your monkey as you see fit, perhaps with a fancy hat if there is a tea party scheduled or a scarf if it's a chilly day.

WAIT A MINUTE, *this monkey needs some friends!*

TYTO *Sock Owl*

One-Sock Wonder

Behind the lenses of his many cameras, Tyto's wide-open eyes take in the whole world. Make sure you have some nice buttons to make his eyes—use a big button behind a smaller button to give them a ringed look.

You'll need

- One sock
- Stuffing
- Scissors, needle, and thread
- Four buttons, two large and two small

DIFFICULTY: *Low*

HOW TO MAKE YOUR OWL

– – – – = sew line
———— = cut line

1. Turn the sock inside out.

2. Cut your sock about ½ inch (12 mm) below the heel. Keep that piece of the sock for the wings and beak. (It can be helpful to draw the pattern on your sock first.)

wing

½ in. (12 mm)

beak

wing

3. Use a **running stitch** (see page 10) to sew a drawstring around the end of the sock, about 1 inch (2.5 cm) from the end.

1 in. (2.5 cm)

4. Gently pull the thread tight. Gather the fabric as you pull so that it folds evenly. Finish with a secure knot.

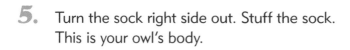

5. Turn the sock right side out. Stuff the sock. This is your owl's body.

6. Use the **overhand stitch** (see page 10) to close the hole. Fold the fabric edges in (toward the inside of the hole) as you sew to make a tidy seam. This is the top of your owl.

7. With the stitches facing you, fold the heel of the sock down over the stitches.

8. Use the overhand stitch to attach the edge of the heel to the body of the owl. Try to keep the ends of the half-moon shape pointy.

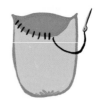

9. Cut the beak shape out of the toe of the sock. Use the overhand stitch to attach it to the face of the owl. Fold the edges under as you sew.

10. Now make your owl's wings with the remaining sock fabric. Make sure the piece is inside out. Use the **backstitch** (see page 10) to sew through both layers of the sock, following the route shown in the picture.

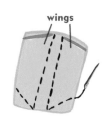

11. Cut out the wings. Turn them right side out.

12. Use the overhand stitch to close the holes. Fold the fabric edge into the hole as you sew.

13. Place the wings on your owl's body. Use the overhand stitch to attach each wing to the body.

14. Now your owl just needs some big eyes! First sew on the larger buttons, following the eye-sewing instructions on page 11.

15. Sew the smaller buttons on top of the larger ones. Just be sure to go through the buttonholes beneath.

TA-DAAAAH! *Now you have an owl to see the sights with.*

CRUSBY SPARKS, PH.D.
Sock Rabbit

Between his scientific research and his quest to perfect his rocket ship, Crusby doesn't have time to dilly-dally. If you're a busy bunny yourself, this is a good animal for you to sew, since it is one of the quickest to make.

You'll need

- Two socks
- Stuffing
- Embroidery floss
- Two or four buttons
- Scissors, needle, and thread

DIFFICULTY: *Medium*

SOCK ONE

- - - - = sew line
———— = cut line

1. Turn the first sock inside out. Lay the sock flat with the heel facing up.

2. To make your rabbit's legs, use the **backstitch** (see page 10) to sew through both layers of the sock, following the route shown in the picture. (It can be helpful to draw the pattern on your sock first.) Leave enough space between the leg seams for easy cutting, and don't sew all the way up to the heel.

legs

3. Cut between the legs to separate them. Be careful not to cut your stitches!

4. Cut the elastic band off the sock.

5. Turn the sock right side out.

6. Stuff your rabbit's body and legs. Is your bunny chubby (more stuffing) or does he have a more athletic build (less stuffing)?

7. Use the **overhand stitch** (see page 10) to sew the large hole shut in a straight line. Fold the fabric edges under (in toward the hole) as you sew so they are hidden.

8. With embroidery floss, use the **satin stitch** (see page 11) to create a nose for your rabbit. You can create a mouth with the backstitch. Does your rabbit have luxuriant whiskers that he tugs while deep in thought? You can add those, too— just tie a knot and leave the thread tail long.

Sock Two

9. Turn the second sock inside out.

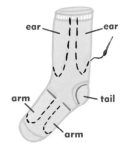

10. Use the backstitch to sew outlines of the arms and ears through both layers of the sock, following the route shown in the picture.

11. Cut out the arms. Turn them right side out, and then stuff them.

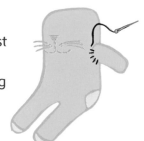

12. Put your rabbit's arms on the sides of the body, just about even with the rabbit's mouth. Use the overhand stitch to attach each arm to the body, folding the fabric edge under as you sew.

13. Cut out the long ears. Turn them right side\out. Fold the stiff elastic band back into each ear. This will help the ears stand up.

14. Position the ears on top of the head, one over each corner. The long vertical seam should be in the back. Use the overhand stitch to attach the ears to the head by sewing around the base of the ear. Pinch the base of the ears slightly while sewing to create a hollow in the front of the ears.

15. Cut out the tail piece from the heel of the sock. Sew the **running stitch** (see page 10) around the edge, but don't tie an ending knot yet. Pull the thread slightly to form a pouch, with the right side of the fabric out.

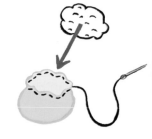

16. Put a little bit of stuffing in the pouch, and then pull the running stitch tight to close the pouch around the stuffing. Tuck the fabric edge into the hole as you pull the thread. Tie a knot, but don't cut the thread.

17. Place the tail on your rabbit's backside with the knot toward the body. Use the overhand stitch to sew the tail to the body.

18. Now sew on your rabbit's button eyes just above his nose, following the eye-sewing instructions on page 11. Just be sure to sew through both sets of button holes if you make double-eyes like the one in the photo.

10, 9, 8, 7, 6, 5 . . .

Time to put on your space suit and join Crusby at the launchpad!

TOOPELO *Sock Elephant*

Most elephants use their trunks to eat, drink, and show their feelings. Toopelo uses her long trunk to decorate umbrellas. Before you attach the trunk to your sock elephant's head, move it up or down, see what it would look like a bit shorter, or try holding it at an angle. Make sure you capture your elephant's mood!

You'll need
- Two socks
- Two buttons
- Stuffing
- Short piece of yarn
- Scissors, needle, and thread

DIFFICULTY: *High*

SOCK ONE

‒ ‒ ‒ ‒ = sew line
———— = cut line

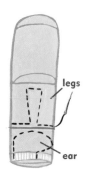

1. Turn the first sock inside out. Lay the sock flat with the heel facing up.

2. To make your elephant's legs and one ear, use the **backstitch** (see page 10) to sew through both layers of the sock, following the route shown in the picture. (It can be helpful to draw the pattern on your sock first.) Don't sew all the way up to the heel. And don't sew the opening of the ear shut.

3. Cut out the ear. Be careful not to cut your stitches! Turn the ear right side out and set it aside.

4. Cut between the legs to separate them.

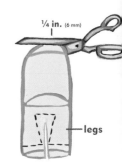

5. Cut off the very tip of the toe of the sock, about ¼ inch (6 mm) in from the tip. You can throw that little scrap away.

6. Now turn the sock right side out through the hole.

7. Add stuffing through this hole. Make sure to get stuffing all the way down in your elephant's legs.

8. Use the **overhand stitch** (see page 10) to sew the hole shut in a straight line. Fold the fabric edges in (toward the inside of the hole) as you sew to make a tidy seam.

Sock Two

9. Turn the second sock inside out.

10. Use the backstitch to sew outlines of the second ear, arms, and trunk, following the route shown in the picture. Do not sew the opening of the ear shut.

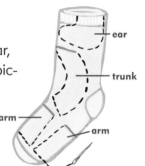

11. Cut out the ear. Turn it right side out. Find the other ear you saved from the first sock.

12. Fold the elastic band back inside each ear.

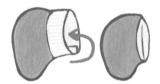

13. To attach the ears, lay one ear flat against your elephant's head. The folded-in edge should lie against the head, facing the front, and the longest part should point down.

14. Use the overhand stitch to sew the folded-in edge to the elephant's head. Repeat with the other ear.

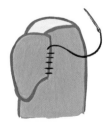

15. Cut out the elephant's arms. Turn them right side out and stuff them.

16. Use the overhand stitch to sew the arms shut. Fold the fabric edges in as you sew.

17. Put your elephant's arms on the sides of the body. Position them at a slight angle down toward the tummy. Use the overhand stitch to attach each arm to the body.

18. Now give your elephant a trunk! Cut the trunk out. Turn it right side out and stuff it.

19. Place the trunk on your elephant. Use the overhand stitch to attach the trunk to the face. Fold the fabric edges under as you sew.

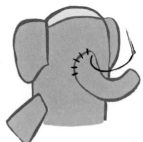

20. Make a tail for your elephant! Cut a piece of yarn about 4 inches (10 cm) long. Tie two knots, each about 1 inch (2.5 cm) from an end of the yarn. Use a needle and thread to sew one of the knots onto your elephant's backside. Fray the other end of the yarn past the hanging knot.

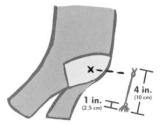

21. Now sew on your elephant's eyes just to the sides of the trunk, following the eye-sewing instructions on page 11.

YOUR ELEPHANT WILL ALWAYS REMEMBER THIS TIME YOU SPENT TOGETHER.

BON ROMPUS
Sock Crocodile

Bon Rompus spends hours laboring over perfect pinch pots, but he himself is pretty easy to make. Do you have any green socks lying about? Find some matching buttons and soon enough you'll have your very own sock croc sneaking around.

You'll need

- Two socks
- Stuffing
- Scissors, needle, and thread
- Two buttons

DIFFICULTY: *High*

SOCK ONE

- - - - = sew line
———— = cut line

1. Turn the first sock inside out.

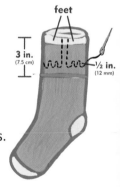

feet

3 in.
(7.5 cm)

½ in.
(12 mm)

2. Use the **backstitch** (see page 10) to sew the outlines of the two front feet, following the route shown in the picture. (It can be helpful to draw the pattern on your sock first.) Make very small stitches as you go around the toes. Each toe should be about ½ inch (12 mm) long.

3. Cut straight across the sock to remove the piece with the feet. Set this piece aside for now.

4. Turn the sock right side out. This will be your crocodile's head and body.

5. Stuff the sock lightly. You can add more stuffing later when the tail is attached.

Sock Two

6. Turn the second sock inside out.

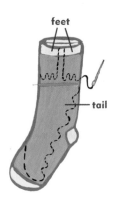

7. Use the backstitch to sew the outlines of the back feet and tail, following the route shown in the picture. (Yay! More tiny croc toes!) Make very small stitches as you go around the toes and the bumps on the tail.

8. Cut straight across the sock to remove the piece with the feet. Set this piece aside with the other feet for now.

9. Cut out the tail. Be careful as you cut around the bumps. Turn it right side out. Make sure you get the bumps, too!

10. Stuff the tail.

11. Position the tail on the body. The bumps of the tail should be on the same side as the heel of Sock One. Use the **overhand stitch** (see page 10) to attach the tail to the body, folding both fabric edges in as you sew to create a tidy seam. Add a bit more stuffing before you finish sewing the pieces together to make sure your croc is evenly stuffed.

12. Make a small knot in the middle of each bump of the tail. This will help the bumps hold their shape.

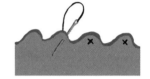

13. Your sock croc needs eyes! Pinch together the fabric of the heel of the sock to make space. Follow the eye-sewing instructions on page 11, and sew your button eyes on through both layers of the heel fabric. Real crocodiles have clever eyes that are the same color as their bodies. What color are your crocodile's eyes?

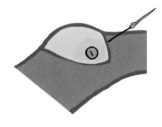

14. Fold the middle top of the heel fabric over. It should slightly overlap the eyes. Use the overhand stitch to sew it to the sock.

15. Put a smile on your crocodile, if he needs it. Or you can skip this optional step. Pinch together two small folds of fabric on one side of your crocodile's long snout. Use a **running stitch** (see page 10) to sew the two folds together. Knot your thread frequently. Sew until you reach the toe of the sock, but don't sew across the toe. Repeat on the other side.

16. Now for the nose. Make a starting knot just below the tip of the nose, in the center. Guide your needle to emerge on the top side of the snout, about 1 inch (2.5 cm) back (toward the eyes) from where you started. Pull this taut to make your crocodile's nose stick up. Sew another knot to anchor the stitch, but don't cut the thread.

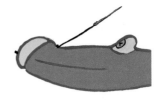

17. Sew back into the nose in the same spot. Guide the needle to come out on the right side of the front of the nose. This will be your crocodile's nostril!

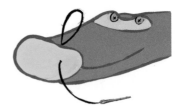

18. Make a horizontal running stitch—but guide your needle to emerge from the same spot on top of the nose, in the middle. Sew a knot.

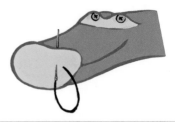

19. Repeat steps 17 and 18 on the left side for the left nostril.

20. Your croc gets from place to place on his tiptoes! Find the feet pieces you sewed earlier, and cut out all four feet. Be sure to cut carefully between the toes. Turn the pieces right side out. Use a chopstick or pencil to make sure the toes are turned all the way out.

21. Fold the elastic band into the feet. Firmly stuff each foot. They should be a bit round.

22. Attach to your crocodile's body using the overhand stitch.

HEY, HE ALREADY SNUCK OFF! *See you later, sock croc maker.* AFTER A WHILE, SOCKODILE.

INKLING *Sock Pig*

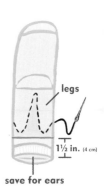

This sock pig's ears are a bit like origami. Be prepared for some tricky folding! If things don't look quite right to you, you can always carefully take out your stitches and try again. Or, if you want simpler ears, follow the pattern for the cat's ears on page 58.

You'll need

- Two socks
- Stuffing
- Scissors, needle, and thread
- Two buttons

DIFFICULTY: *Highest*

SOCK ONE

‑ ‑ ‑ ‑ = sew line
——— = cut line

1. Turn the first sock inside out. Lay the sock flat with the heel facing up.

2. To make your pig's pointy legs, use the **backstitch** (see page 10) to sew through both layers of the sock, following the route shown in the picture. (It can be helpful to draw the pattern on your sock first.) Leave enough space between the leg seams for easy cutting, and don't sew all the way up to the heel. Don't sew closer than 2 inches (5 cm) to the opening of the sock.

legs

1½ in. (4 cm)

save for ears

3. Cut off the elastic band about 1½ inches (4 cm) from the opening of the sock. Set it aside; you will need it later.

4. Cut between the legs to separate them. Be careful not to cut your stitches!

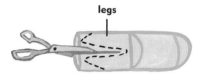

legs

5. Turn the sock over, so the heel faces down. *Through the top layer only*, make a short horizontal cut about 1½ inches (4 cm) below the tip of the toe of the sock. Later, you'll sew your pig's snout on top of this hole, so leave room for the snout and the eyes above it.

1½ in.
(4 cm)

6. Now turn the sock right side out through the hole you just cut.

7. Add stuffing through this hole. Make your pig as plump as you'd like.

8. Use the **overhand stitch** (see page 10) to sew the hole shut.

SOCK TWO

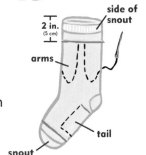

9. Turn the second sock inside out.

10. Use the backstitch to sew the arms and tail through both layers of the sock, following the route shown in the picture.

11. Make the pig's snout! Cut off the toe portion of the sock about 2 inches (5 cm) down from the tip. Turn the toe right side out.

12. Stuff the toe.

13. Cut off the elastic band about 2 inches (5 cm) from the opening of the sock. Turn it right side out.

14. Place the elastic band around the stuffed toe of the sock. Both of their unfinished fabric edges should be on the same side, where you can see the stuffing.

15. Use the overhand stitch to attach the front edge of the elastic band to the toe of the sock. Try to keep the toe of the sock somewhat flat as you sew.

16. Place the snout over the hole on the body. Starting on either side of the snout, use the overhand stitch to attach the snout to the body. As you are stitching, shape the underside of the snout so that it is a little higher at the middle.

17. When you have stitched all the way around, stitch a knot to anchor but don't cut the thread.

18. Make some nostrils for your pig! Guide your needle under the snout from the edge, emerging on the front of the snout, a bit off center.

19. Make a short horizontal stitch on one side of the front of the snout.

20. Guide the needle back through the snout and exit at the middle of the lower edge of the snout, where the snout meets the body. Pull the thread taut to make the nostril dimple. Stitch a knot to anchor, but do not cut your thread.

21. Repeat for the other nostril. This time, exit at the other side of the snout, sew a knot, and cut the thread. The snout is finished!

22. Carefully cut out the arms. Turn them right side out and stuff them.

23. Use the overhand stitch to attach the arms to the sides of the body, just below the snout. Fold the fabric edges under as you sew.

24. Now make your pig a pair of cute little ears. Cut the remaining elastic band into two pieces. Trim the pieces to be about 2½ inches (6 cm) long each.

25. Fold the unfinished edges over themselves and use a **running stitch** (see page 10) to hem them.

├──── 2½ in. ────┤
(6 cm)

26. Place a strip with the hem facing up. Fold the two corners of one short side toward each other so the corners meet, as you would when making a paper airplane.

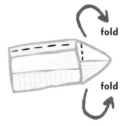

fold

fold

27. Now fold the strip in half lengthwise. Use the overhand stitch to sew the two diagonal folded edges together. This is the tip of your pig's ear.

28. Place one ear on your pig's head, near the very top. The open side should face front.

29. Keep the base of the ear curved. Use the overhand stitch to attach it to the head.

30. Fold your pig's ear so it points forward. Make a couple of running stitches on each side of the ear to hold this shape.

31. Repeat steps 26 through 30 to make the other ear.

32. Wait! Where's the pig's tail? Cut out the tail piece from Sock Two. Be careful not to cut your stitches. Turn the tail right side out.

33. Sew a loose running stitch through both layers of fabric down the middle all the way from the tip to the base of the pig's tail. Do not tie a knot.

34. Pull on the thread while gently holding the base of the tail. As the fabric gathers, help it form into a curl. Stitch a knot, but don't cut the thread.

35. Use the overhand stitch to attach the tail to the pig's backside. Fold the fabric edges under as you sew.

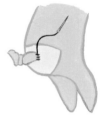

36. Attach two button eyes to the body just above the snout, following the eye-sewing instructions on page 11.

If only your pig had a field of folded paper flowers to frolic in!

MINNIE WIMZY
Sock Squirrel

Can Minnie bake a perfect acorn pie? Yes! And she will be happy to share it with you. Can you make this squirrel with just one sock? Yes! She's small, and there are some tricky steps to complete this little squirrel, but don't worry—you can do it.

You'll need

- One sock
- Stuffing
- Scissors, needle, and thread
- Two or four coordinating buttons

DIFFICULTY: Highest

HOW TO MAKE YOUR SQUIRREL

- - - - = sew line
───── = cut line

1. Turn the sock inside out. Lay the sock flat with the heel facing up.

2. To make your squirrel's short little legs, use the **backstitch** (see page 10) to sew through both layers of sock, following the route shown in the picture. (It can be helpful to draw the pattern on your sock first.)

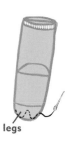

legs

3. Cut off the top of the sock about 1½ inches (4 cm) above the heel (below the band). Keep this piece to make the squirrel's tail.

1½ in.
(4 cm)

legs

4. Cut between the legs to separate them. Be careful not to cut your stitches!

5. Turn the sock right side out. Use your fingers or the end of a wooden spoon to make sure the legs are turned all the way out.

6. Add some stuffing through the large hole at the top. Be sure to get the stuffing down into the legs, but don't stuff the body too firmly near the opening.

7. Use the **overhand stitch** (see page 10) to sew the large hole shut in a straight line. Fold the fabric into the hole as you sew so they are hidden.

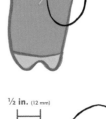

8. To make your squirrel's ears, fold the middle of this sewn edge over the heel of the sock. Starting about ½ inch (12 mm) in from the corner, use the overhand stitch to sew the top edge down. Stop when you are about ½ inch (12 mm) from the other end. The little ends that stick up are the ears!

½ **in.** (12 mm)

9. Now make your squirrel's front paws. Pinch together about 1 inch (2.5 cm) of fabric just under your squirrel's chin. Try to get some stuffing in there, too. Make a starting knot at the base of the pinched fabric in the middle. Make sure you have at least ½ inch (12 mm) to work with.

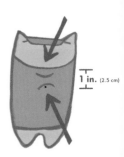

1 **in.** (2.5 cm)

10. Guide the needle in at the base and out at the top of where you are pinching. Be careful not to sew into the heel of the sock. Repeat this stitch once in the same place (in at the bottom, out at the top).

11. Pull the stitch snug. This forms your squirrel's little front paws. Sew a knot to keep the stitch tight, but don't cut the thread.

12. Put your thumb under the squirrel's chin, and put your index and middle fingers on either side of the seam on top of the squirrel's head. Squeeze slightly to flatten the head.

13. Starting from the underside of the paws, guide your needle through the heel of the sock up through the top stitching, between your fingers and centered on the seam. Be careful not to poke yourself!

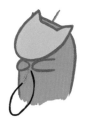

14. Carefully dive the needle back into the fabric about ⅛ inch (4 mm) down the back of your squirrel's head, emerging under the paws. Keep the thread slightly taut to create a squirrelly hunch. Sew a knot!

⅛ in.
(4 mm)

15. Now make the arms. Pinch together about 1 inch (2.5 cm) of the fabric to the left of the paws. Use the **running stitch** (see page 10) to sew behind where your fingers are pinching. Keep the stitches tight.

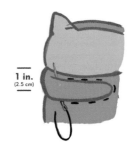

1 in.
(2.5 cm)

16. Repeat to the right of the paws.

17. Now make your squirrel's face! Make a starting knot in the heel of the sock, just above where the paws meet. (Don't cut the thread until you're all done with the squirrel's face, after step 23.)

18. Pinch the sides of the bottom half of your squirrel's face together so that there is extra fabric above the knot. Poke the extra fabric in so that it is hidden in the fold between the two cheeks.

19. Hold the cheeks together. Use the overhand stitch to sew the two cheeks together. Sew a knot about ½ inch (12 mm) up the heel.

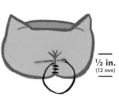

½ in.
(12 mm)

20. To create a nose, make a vertical stitch about ¼ inch (6 mm) on the left side of the small crease at the top of the seam you just created. Pull the stitch tight to accent the nose shape and tie a knot.

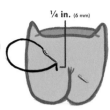
¼ **in.** (6 mm)

21. Repeat on the right side of the crease.

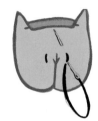

22. Begin a small horizontal stitch across the bridge of the nose, poking your needle into the stuffed animal. Guide your needle down and out again to emerge at the base of the cheek seam.

23. Keep the thread slightly taut. Sew a knot to secure. Now you can cut the thread!

24. What kind of eyes does your squirrel have? Big bulgy eyes or small beady eyes? We like to use a smaller button on top of a slightly larger button for an observant look. Attach a button to the left of your squirrel's nose, following the eye-sewing instructions on page 11.

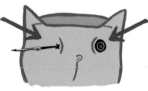

25. Pinch the sides of your squirrel's face together and carefully guide the needle through to where the other eye will be. Sew a knot to keep the face slightly pinched.

26. Attach the other button eye. Make sure it is level with the first eye.

27. Finally, give that squirrel a bushy tail! With the remaining piece of the sock inside out, back-stitch the outline of the tail through both layers of fabric.

tail

28. Cut out the shape and turn it right side out. Stuff the tail.

29. Place the tail on your squirrel's back. Use the overhand stitch to sew up one side of the tail where it meets the back and then down the other and across the bottom.

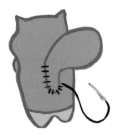

MAKE AN APRON FOR MINNIE WIMZY!

An apron is a good place for her to dust the flour off her tiny hands. She likes to be tidy. Find a small piece of fabric or felt or a very small doily, and cut it into a half-circle. Hold it up to your squirrel's tummy to see if the piece is about the right size for an apron. Trim it to make it smaller if needed. Now find a piece of ribbon that is long enough to go around Minnie's waist twice. Sew the straight edge of the fabric to the back side of the ribbon, right in the middle. That's it! Now tie the apron on Minnie, and it's pie time

Now go bake an acorn pie with Minnie!

SOLIS IPSY *Sock Cat*

Your sock cat is designed with a sewn-on muzzle, but you could embroider a nose instead if you want to do a bit less sewing. Take a look at the sock rabbit on page 23 to see directions for making an embroidered face. You know what they say: there's more than one way to grin a cat.

You'll need

- Two socks
- Stuffing
- Two buttons
- Scissors, needle, and thread

DIFFICULTY: *High*

SOCK ONE

- - - - = sew line
———— = cut line

1. Turn the first sock inside out. Lay the sock flat with the heel facing up.

2. To make your cat's legs, use the **backstitch** (see page 10) to sew through both layers of the sock, following the route shown in the picture. (It can be helpful to draw the pattern on your sock first.) Leave enough space between the leg seams for easy cutting, and don't sew all the way up to the heel. Don't sew closer than 2 inches (5 cm) to the opening of the sock.

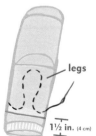

legs

1½ in. (4 cm)

3. Cut off the elastic band of the sock about 1½ inches (4 cm) from the end and set it aside to use later. Cut between the legs to separate them. Be careful not to cut your stitches!

4. Cut off the toe of the sock.

5. Now, turn the sock right side out through the hole.

6. Add stuffing through this hole. Make sure to get stuffing all the way down into your cat's legs.

7. Use the **overhand stitch** (see page 10) to sew the hole shut in a straight line. Fold the fabric edges in (toward the inside of the hole) as you sew to make a tidy seam.

SOCK TWO

8. Turn the second sock inside out. Lay the sock flat with the heel facing up.

9. Use the backstitch to sew outlines of the tail, ears, nose, and arms through both layers of the sock. Try to make the ears as big as you can, but the nose should only be about ¾ inch (2 cm) wide. Try to make the arms the same length as the legs were on the other sock.

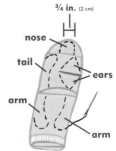

¾ in. (2 cm)

nose

tail

ears

arm

arm

10. Cut out the ears. Turn them right side out. Use the overhand stitch to sew the holes shut. Fold the fabric edges in as you sew.

11. Place each ear on the diagonal behind a corner of your cat's head.

12. Using the overhand stitch, sew along the bottom edge of the ear on the back of the cat's head. When you get to the front, sew along the edge of the cat's head.

13. Cut out the nose. Turn it right side out. Set it aside for a moment.

14. To start your cat's muzzle, get the elastic band you set aside from Sock One. Cut it so it lays flat. Now trim it so it is about 4 inches (10 cm) long.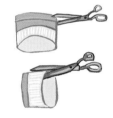

— 4 in. (10 cm) —

15. Use the backstitch to hem the cut fabric edge. Round the two corners on that seam by folding them in as you sew.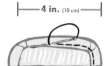

16. Lay the elastic band in front of you with the stitched side facing you and the rounded corners on the bottom. Lay the reserved nose piece in the middle of the strip.

17. Use the overhand stitch to attach the nose to the muzzle. The top of the nose should be even with the top edge of the muzzle.

18. Place this piece on the body where your cat's face should be. Fold the left side of the elastic strip in and down across the nose, and then fold the right side the same way. The two sides should overlap slightly. Make any adjustments that seem necessary—should the muzzle be wider or narrower, or should it cover the nose more?

19. Use the overhand stitch to sew around the edges of the muzzle.

20. Now sew on your cat's eyes just to the sides of the muzzle, following the eye-sewing instructions on page 11.

21. Cut out the arms from the sock. Turn them right side out and stuff them.

22. Pinch the hole into a straight line perpendicular to the seam. Use the overhand stitch to sew the hole shut. Fold the fabric edges in as you sew.

23. Put an arm on each side of the body. Use the overhand stitch to attach each arm to the body.

24. Cut out the tail. Turn it right side out and stuff it. Because the tail is skinny, it is easier to stuff if you use small bits of stuffing.

25. Use the overhand stitch to attach the tail to the cat's backside. Fold the fabric edges in as you sew.

WHAT'S THAT, MEOW?
Oh, yes, I think it is time for a milk bath!

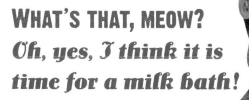

TAT RUTABAGA

Sock Bear

If your socks are big, you might be able to make Tat Rutabaga out of just one. His legs are pretty short! Try cutting the pattern out of paper first, and then lay the pieces on a large sock to see if they will fit. Maybe you could make a pair of bears!

You'll need

- Two socks
- Stuffing
- One dark four-hole button
- Two small buttons or beads
- Scissors, needle, and thread

DIFFICULTY: *High*

SOCK ONE

- - - - = sew line
———— = cut line

1. Turn the first sock inside out. Lay it flat with the heel facing up.

2. To make your bear's legs, use the **backstitch** (see page 10) to sew through both layers of the sock, following the route shown in the picture. (It can be helpful to draw the pattern on your sock first.) Don't sew all the way up to the heel. Your bear's legs should be shorter than his body by about half.

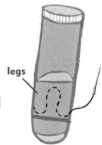

legs

3. Cut around and between the legs. Be careful not to cut your stitches!

4. Cut the elastic band off the top of the sock and discard.

5. Now turn the sock right side out through the open end. Use your fingers or the end of a wooden spoon to make sure the legs are turned all the way out.

6. Add stuffing. Is your bear rather rotund? Make sure you get plenty of stuffing in there!

7. Use the **overhand stitch** (see page 10) to sew the hole shut in a straight line. Fold the fabric edges into the hole as you sew, to hide them.

SOCK TWO

8. Turn the second sock inside out.

9. Use the backstitch to sew the outlines of the ears, arms, and tail, following the route shown in the picture. Your bear's arms should be a little longer than his legs.

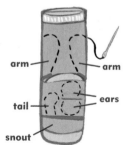

arm
arm
tail
ears
snout

10. Cut off the toe portion of the sock about 3 inches (7.5 cm) down from the tip. Turn the toe right side out. This will be your bear's snout.

3 in.
(7.5 cm)

11. Find the two little lines that run up the sides of the toe. Fold the toe so these lines almost meet at the top and are about 1 inch (2.5 cm) apart where the toe seam is. To make this easier, place the toe of the sock over your index and ring fingers with the toe seam facing you. Use your other hand to push the fabric into the space between your two fingers.

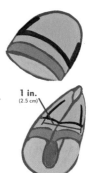

1 in.
(2.5 cm)

12. Use the overhand stitch to sew along the crease where the two folds meet. Leave a small gap at the top.

13. Time to put on your bear's nose! Make a starting knot in the small gap from the previous step. Place a four-hole button over the needle and position it inside the gap. The bottom of the button should be slightly covered by the fabric folds.

14. Attach the button to the snout by sewing from the button's top right hole into the bottom right hole, then crossing behind the button to keep the thread hidden, and sewing from the top left hole into the bottom left hole. This way, only the vertical stitches show on the front of the button. They look like nostrils.

15. Repeat step 14 until the button is secure. Tie a knot behind the button, but do not cut the thread.

16. Starting from the back of the button, guide your needle out through the bottom right hole and into the top right hole and up through the top of the snout.

17. Now sew a short stitch across the top of the snout, down through the fabric, out the top left hole of the button and back in through the bottom left hole of the button. (This gives your bear a little turned-up nose and helps the button stay inside the gap.)

18. Keep the thread taut and tie a knot behind the button.

19. Stuff your bear's snout.

20. Position the snout on the bear's body. The seam from the fold should be on the underside of the snout. Use the overhand stitch to attach the snout to the body, folding the fabric edge under as you sew.

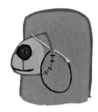

21. Cut out the arms. Turn them right side out and stuff them. Sew the holes shut with the overhand stitch, folding the edges of fabric in as you sew.

22. Put your bear's arms on the sides of the body, slightly lower than the snout. Use the overhand stitch to attach each arm to the body. The arms should hang slightly forward and down.

23. Cut out the ears. Turn them right side out.

24. Position the ears over the corners of the head. The corner will be inside the ear. Use the overhand stitch to sew around the base of the ears, folding the fabric edge under as you sew.

25. Cut out the tail. Turn it right side out.

26. Put your bear's tail on the back of the body. Use the overhand stitch to attach the tail to the body, folding the fabric edge under as you sew.

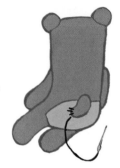

27. Sew two beady little eyes on near the snout, following the eye-sewing instructions on page 11.

NOW YOUR BEAR JUST NEEDS A TINY MANDOLIN *and a happy little tune to play!*

Other Sock Creatures You Can Make

Well, now you know how to make a sock monkey and a few other sock animals. The basic techniques that you learned here—shaping ears, sewing arms, curling tails, and so on—can help you create new sock friends. Is there a yawning sock hippo in your future? A school of gifted fish? An extra-alert dachshund? Or will you dream up your own creature? Invent, create, sew! The sock animal itself is really just a bonus; the fun is in the doing.

MEET MORE
Sock Friends!

Post *your* sock creations to the **Sock Friends Gallery** at http://monkeysockmonkey.com.